Life After Abuse

This story will impact the life's of hurting women all over the world.To let them know there is life after abuse.We may not understand why we are being abused by the man that took a vow to love us for better or worse. But one thing we need to know is how will we put up with abuse. As I took a look at this abuse I found out abuse would be passed down from generations of men. My husband great grandfather abused his wife,which caused three generations of abuse. On my side of the family my grandfather was abusive to my grandmother, and my father was abusive to my mother. I want this abuse to stop with me. No more Abuse!

Words of my daughter: November 12, 2004
My Inspiration
I've been through so many things in my life thus far and there's only one person who has been present with me all these years. Someone who I can trust and that i know will never leave me for any reason what so ever. This person is very special to me and I look up to them very much. Who am I talking about? My mother. She is my best friend because I cantalk to her about anything. We

are practically inseparable. I cannot stand to be away from her. If I go tomy friends house I cannot go to bed unless I talk to her first, just to make sure she's ok. I never thought that my mother would influence my life so much. When i was 8 years old my mother left my father because of issues they had in their marriage. At first i hated my mother for leaving my father only because I missed him. I didn't really interact with her for days, just stayed in my room and kept to myself. Now that I am older I understand why things that happened when I was younger really happened. Some women believe that things in their marriage will get better but they never do so they just choose to endure what ever the situation may be. Some stay because they are scared to be alone and are incapable of doing without the one they have loved for so long no matter how much it may hurt them. Not my mother, she felt that it was in her kid's best interest to do what she did and that is what I most respect about her. "No matter what someone may say negative about you don't believe it because it's not really his or her way of trying to control you, is what she tells me. I know that all throughout my life there are going to be times when people have negative things to say but I know to keep my head held high only not to submit to those things. When i was 10 years old my mother did something that would change our lives forever. She took up guardianship for five of my cousins. My cousins mother and father gave my mother full grardianship of their five children, ranging in ages from 8 to 3 at the time, until they could get some help for their problems. Its been almost nine years and my mother cares for eight children; my brother and sister, my five cousins and me. At first it was fun but the reality became real. My oldest cousin is blind he couldn't do much of anything, My mother got him into Texas school for the Blind in Austin and now he reads Braille on almost a college level and is only in the tenth grade. The other four had never been to school and all had ADHD, one was even dyslectic. You really wouldn't know it today if you see them; they're more controlled than they use to be. She has been through so many hardships with them from getting them into school to doctor's appointment. Never once did she just give up and say forget this. She had to work three jobs at one point just to care for us, but nerve complained once. From this she thought me never to give up on anything, especially when it gets hard. Anything you can endure and it doesn't kill you only makes you stronger. Also she thought me how to help people who really need you . If it hadn't been for my mom who knows where my cousins would be. I think that's why I'm always trying to help out someone in his or her time of need any way I can. Now my mother has started her own non-profit called Family Fight Against HIV/AIDS, Inc. She does HIV/AIDS awareness outreach services.She passes out pamphlets on the disease where she feels it would do the most good in the communities. She went back to school to become a drug counselor. She has accomplished so much in such a small period of time and still has time to support all of her kids. She makes time to spend with all of us and me being a senior she tries to come to everything I participate in. I just have so much respect for her and the things she does. Mostly I just respect our relation because most of my friends don't get along with their mothers and always tell me that they wish they had the type of relationship we have, so I know not to take mine for granted. What they don't know that this relationship was 18 years in the making and is still going. It's not perpect but that's where all the learning experiences come from.

There are 6 types of Abuse
1) Physical Abuse
2) Emotional Abuse
3)Verbal Abuse
4)Economic Abuse
5) Mental Abuse
6) Sexual Abuse

Domestic Violence

Barriers caused by cultural religious beliefs- linguistic barrier, Isolation from home/family also adopted community. Guided by values of privacy honor loyalty shame,Total dependency on one person ie the Abuser, Lack of knowledge of legal rights and resources.

Harris County has the highest number of deaths in state followed by Dallas, Tarrant, Bexar, El Paso, Hidalgo.

Statistics on Domestic Violence

Globally 1 out of 3 women are beaten or sexually abused during their life time.
US Approximately 3 Million women battered every year.

US approximately 10 Million children are exposed to domestic violence each year.

Texas 182,087 incidents reported in 2004.

Houston 31,000 incidents in 2004.

Harris County over 45,000 Family violence incidents reported in an average year.

In Texas 114 women were killed due to domestic violence murder by their husband, ex-husband, intimate partner, boyfriend, or ex-boyfriend ages of women 15 yrs - 84 yrs.

30% deaths Harris County

74% women killed at home

60% shot

17% stabbed

11% strangled

21% women take steps to leave

20% homicides within one to two days of a national holiday

15% by standers or witnesses killed

4% bodies burned

2012 there were 38,490 incidents of domestic violence reported in Harris County

26% of all Texas female intimate homicides occurred in Harris County 2012

30 women were killed in 2012 Harris County due to Domestic Violence

2009 Houston Police Dept. alone tallied 27,214 reported incidents of Domestic Violence

12,356 adults received shelter from their abusive relationship

16,968 children received shelter

Domestic Violence of men

1 in 6 men suffer from domestic violence in their life time. In 2014 4% of men had experienced domestic violence this is an estimated of 600,000 male victims

Can you imagine feeling like being in the hole in the wall more than church? Thats the feeling I got when I met DJ Black. Look at them wrangler jeans, thats what caught my eye. He had me mesmerized, how could this be? I would be found in church at the age of 4. I could remember living next door to Oak Baptist Church I was always excited about going to church service. I didn't wait for my father or mother to take me to church. I got dressed and took myself. I came from a middle class family we lived in a house on 2 acres of land I had four brother, my mother was a domestic caregiver and my father drove a dump truck and owed a bar. I loved my grandmother so much i would cry to go with her to work. I had a good life at the age of 6 to 8 my mother left my father he was abusive and cheated on her, I'm the oldest child of 13 children of my fathers children. My mother had enough of his abuse and cheating so she took me and my brothers and moved out. We moved to a place called Link City apartments (the ghetto) never had we seen this type of living, there was stealing and killing. My brothers and I had to learn how to fight as little children this was not good, the children in the (ghetto) were fighters. We were use to playing in our club house in our old neighborhood. This was a different type of environment for us, we ended up living there one year. My mother found her father in Hitch Town we moved there and stayed there for one year. The last move my mother took was to Sugar Town. We stayed there for the rest of our youth life. In Sugar Town at the age of 11 I would give my life to the Lord. I joined Fresh Baptist Church where I was baptized by Pastor James. I became a faithful member there where I serviced on the usher board, choir, working to do what ever the church needed me to do. As a member of this church I got to spend a lot of time with Pastor James, Sister James and their children, I was part of their family. I got to see the love that Pastor James had for Sister James they had real love for each other. As the years passed by I got more involved with things of the church every time the church doors opened I was there. Now at the age of 17 the devil had a plan for me. I started hanging out with some of my friends from school. We started to hang out in the hole in the wall in Rich Town they didn't care about our age. Going out to the hole in the wall would change my will to go to church.This was not a good thing but back than I didn't know that. I was starting to move on a different path into darkness. Church started to be the last place that I wanted to be. The hole in wall was where I wanted to be with my friends hanging out every night.When I graduated from high school I was happy cause it was time for me to move out of my mothers house. Pastor James said to me "Take this time to stay at your mothers house and go to collage" I said "no way im moving out" so I did. I should have listened to Pastor James because I had roommates not a good idea everything was in my name after one month of living there they made plans to move out with their boyfriend left me to pay all the bills not cool. Out of school I became a hair stylist working for Dino's of Houston traveling all over the U.S. doing hair shows. I continued to hang out at the hole in the wall. This night at the hole in the wall, I met DJ Black we started spending time together away from the bar because Black was a playboy but I still wanted that man. 'He was hot'. Meeting Black would change my life. Two years into the relationship I got pregnant and I told Black after sometime Black asked me to marry him I said yes I will! So we found us a apartment to move into, baby was born September 6, 1986, two months after I had the baby we got married at court house on November 21, 1986, Black was 8 years older than me. This marriage would change my life forever. The next 8 years I would live a life of domestic violence.

The first type abuse I experienced was Physical Abuse About two months into the marriage Black came home upset about something and we had words he hit me, I was in shock I told him never to hit me again. This is not what a marriage suppose to be like. Two months went by and he came home upset yelling at me he hit me again I took a candle holder hit him back in his face and he said BITCH if I'm bleeding I will kill you he tried to but I got away we stopped the bleeding so he could go to ER when we got there he told me to stay in car. When he came out he had 4 stitches in his face, this scar would stay with him for life. Being abused by my husband is not what I expected to be doing in this marriage this would lead up to years of domestic violence. The third time he hit me I left walking with my baby to my brothers house where I would spend the night the next day I went back home he was gone to work I didn't know what to expect by going back but it was ok. After the third time I lost count of the times we would have domestic violence going on at our house the police would come but they would tell one of us to leave come back the next day. I found out in time that Black was drinking, druging with his friends running women. If there was a full moon and Black was drinking it was a fight. Two years into the marriage I got pregnant with my second child he said to me we cant afford another child so we will get rid of it. The next fight we had he hit me in the stomach so than I said he killed my baby so I got the abortion, him and his friend took me downtown to have it done, this is what he wanted me to get done this was not my decision to kill my baby this would upset me for years to come. I said that GOD will not forgive me for that but as my husband he was head of the house and he made the decision without me or GOD! This was painful me for years to come not knowing if it was a boy or girl this joy taking from me. I had to ask GOD to forgive me for years. The cheating started after that my oldest could talk good at 3 she said to me on phone May is here at our house! What was she doing at my house if Im at work he was not to have another women in our house without me being there. They had been to a party for our niece so Black said to May let me show you where I live this was not acceptable. By the time I hang up the phone and made it to his mother house they were there so I didn't say anything to them but they knew that it was wrong. I would be alienated from my family and friends, My best friend was Jane she would always tell me everything is going to be alright. We went out one night to the club in Rich Town we came back from club about 3:00 am and had to pick up children from my mothers house so I would get home about 4:30 am Black was mad he took a baseball bat and hit me on my leg I didn't have feeling in that spot for years it was like a blockage there. The next thing that happened to me I had a pain in chest at work theytook me to the ER and they ran tests on I was there in the hospital for five days. I had two blood clot that past through my heart and stopped in my lungs, Black didn't take the time out to come see me in the hospital only my mother and his mother came to see me, his mother gave me a ride home. The next day he was mad and he began to choke me to death but I got up, the next day my neck and face was black and blue I had to go to work like this, my manager said to me one day that man will kill you I said no he want. The domestic violence got worse he started coming to my job with mess we would call police but he would drive off.

The second type abuse that I experienced was Mental Abuse. Black would try to turn the table on me saying I'm cheating on him with the truck drivers at my job I'm at work what time do I have to cheat. One night he came home mad he put a gun to my head saying that he would kill me! I just prayed to GOD, he would hide his clothes behind toilet asking me who been in my house no answer was right he still wanted to fight I had so many hits to the head black eyes I cant tell you. Black would take me to work and would not come back to get me for days as if this was ok in my car. I had to find a ride home get baby from my mothers house get back to work the next day. I was never able to catch Black cheating on me for myself but my friends would see in the act of cheating some would tell me, but some would say that's not my business. My friends talked to some of the girls that he had taking to my house while i was at work. I did find some numbers in his beeper back then we didn't have cell phones just beeper I would call only to got their children so I hang up.

The third type of abuse that I experienced was Sexually Abuse. If I was sleep and he came in and wanted sex I would have to give it to him. Even if he had been gone for days. One night he came home drunk raped me from the Anus with no lubricant I was in pain upset crying asking him to stop! He raped me two times from the anus this was very painful, degrading loss of respect for him as my husband, this was the man that I took a vow to love for better or worse. I tried very hard to stay in my marriage but it takes both of us working together giving 100% to each. Now when your married and you say NO this means the husband should respect the wife when she says NO! It does not mean cause I'm your wife you got to give it to me, at this point that is Rape married or not! NO IS NO!

The foruth type of abuse was Economic Abuse, Black worked as a security guard he said for a whole year that he didn't get paid went to work everyday how could this be. I was dumb as hell believing this lie. I had to work two job for us to make it. As the head of the house he should have had two jobs. I let this take place I didn't understand the power I had in me to pray. It would take me 5 years to get pregnant with my 3 child than 18 months after that I got pregnant with my 4th child . Then from there the cheating started to get worse we were separated 3 times before but I took him back time after time trying to make the marriage work. In my mind i thought that i could change this man to love me and change the way he threat his wife. After 8 years of Blacks abuse I made up my mind to take my children and leave him for good no going back for me. I moved out to the getto as I called it cause there I had to become a (ghetto) mother fighting to protect me and my children. For 6 month straight my lights would be cut off no help from Black. I would make sure that my children were feed there was a place where I could get them a burger for 99 cent so $3 could feed them every night I didn't have to eat but they did that is what a good mother do to take care of her babies. I would end up working two job to care for my children my children!

After I left Black this is when I would see him with a women at his mothers house this lady was named Lynn. Black said to me don't act up I said what but act up I had to ask God to give me strength cause I wanted to whip all their asses! Black's mother knew all the time that Black was cheating she should not have allowed him to bring other women to her house cause he was a married man. I left to go to my job interview after I came back they had left the mother asked me are you ok I said yes but I was mad as hell, I just seen my husband with another women. It would be her truck that he would drive home time to time. He even had the nerve to give me a ride in her truck, I didn't ask questions on who truck it was. I never said anything to Lynn about being with my husband. I would often see them riding in the truck going to work. She had gotten him a good job with her at the Post Offices and he nerver gave me money for the children. I kept praying to God and in five years she died of cancer but before she died Lynn got to see Black from my eyes she catch him in the flee market with Joy and many more. I don't know why Lynn would think that Black would not cheat on her, he was another women husband you reap what you sow. Two months after Lynn died Black had a stroke he had to call Lo (his wife) to ask me to bring my children to see him in the hospital. I asked the children if they wanted to see him in the hospital they said no. I thought that it could be a chance that he would get his life together for the children but that didn't happen.After he got better he became the playboy again.Black moved in with his new girl friend her name was Joy she had three children of her own but Black never tried to get the children to spin time with them.

Let me turn back for a minute when I left Black I was hurt had pain in my soul. I would start to mess around with 10 different men all around the city, some of them were married I didn't care, some I didn't know their name if one acted up I wouldn't see them for two weeks I could do that because I was in charge of my self. When your in pain you cause pain to others. I was hurt and in pain for years to come I would begin to party more and more and kept looking for love in all the wrong places. I would take the man as he was he didn't have to have a job as long as he loved me for what i thought love was some didn't know what real love was they would all in up cheating and i would find out and dump they, I had no time to play games. I had to allow God to come back in my life i started to go back to church.To seek God with all my heart cause this was not a life for me and my children.

After all this Black would not file for a divorce I had to file and pay 650.00 to be freed. God showed me that he was trying to do something in my life it was time to let go, And let God. I was able to get my divorce after 21 years of staying married to Black. I had to forgive him for all the things he did to me.I had to be crafty in order to get Black to sign the divorce papers so i stop off by the soul food place to get two oxil tales dinners, i called Black to see if he was at work, he was so i told him that i needed him to sign some papers. I explained that God was tring to use me and i need to be free from him and maybe God can syart to use him. When God is moving you have to move to. I only stayed free for one month I got married to my husband now.

Than in 6 months God called me into ministry to preach his word. When there is a call on your life from God he will see that you make it to get in a place with him as he began to speak to you. Some time we can take the wrong road that led us the wrong master. But if we put our focus on God he will help us to make it back to him.

If I wouldn't truly forgive Black for all the wrong he did to me God could not have used me for his glory. Black had cancer in his mouth and he had it removed it took a

team of 5 doctors for this surgery. This surgery would change Blacks appearance for good he would never look the same again. I went to the hospital to see Black what I saw was not good. Black would have a two year fight for his life, as time went by he would have many different types of surgery's, the doctor had to reconstruct his face and mouth this was not a easy process when your use to eating and talking with out trouble he was growing weak and tried. Black had a feeding tube to eat and drink this caused him to lose 100 pounds or more. Black had to write what he wanted to say. He could not drive his self anymore. The last time I went with the children to the hospital to see their father. Joy was there and her three children me and my three children, Joy asked Black if he wanted me to pray he answerd yes I prayed that God will would be done. I prayed on Saturday on Monday God called Black home. By Tuesday he was cremated by Wednesday about 3 am God showed me in a dream that his soul made it to heaven. Only because of forgiveness God was able to show me this. We have to know that we are not the judge GOD is the only one to judge us AMEN
When you have forgiveness it is the intertional and voluntary process by which a victim under goes a change feeling and attitude. You have to truely forgive for God and your self.

There are 6 types of Abuse
Physical Abuse
Emotional Abuse
Verbal Abuse
Economic Abuse
Mental Abuse
 Sexual Abuse

Physical Abuse - standing over you getting in your face grabbing you if you try to leave kicking punching biting slapping choking threatening to harm you using weapons, throwing things, breaking things, punching walls or doors, driving recklessly, burning, cutting, pulling hair, stabbing, strangling tying or confining you, preventing you, from seeking medical care, murder

Mental Abuse - Playing mind games with you twisting around so nothing is their fault and all of their behavior was caused by something you did or didn't do. Accusing you of doing things that they are doing, lying, manipulating you for control or sex threatening to out you to parents, friend, classmate, distorting reality so you think you are losing your mind

Sexual Abuse - Rape unwanted sexual touching, vulgar comments pressure for sex forcing you to have unprotected sex forcing you to get pregnant or to have an abortion, sexting forcing you to have sex with other people or to watch your partner have sex with someone else, forcing you to use or participate in pornography

Emotional Abuse - insults, putdown intimidating you, embarrassing you in public talking down to you not listening to or respecting your feeling making threats telling you, that you're not worth anything, being jealous, possessive, controlling excessive or threatening

Verbal Abuse - yelling, shouting, swearing, continuously arguing, talking over you putting you down using threatening language name calling

Economic Abuse - withholding money, acting a fool at your job , not getting paid, preventing you from using the car, not picking you up from work in your own car

In relationship abuse is a pattern of abusive and coecive behaviors used to maintain power and control over a former or current intimate partner. If you are being abused by your husband or boy friend you may feel confused, angry, afraid, trapped and not knowing what to do to get out of the relationship. We as the abused think that we are the reason of the abuse but no one should have the power to keep you in a abusive relationship. We must start to think of our self and not put up with this abuse. We put our children and some family members at risk of being harmed. We have to take a stand and say no more Abuse. If more people would take a stand to do the right thing when it come to seeing someone abused and say no don't do that it would be a better place here on earth. Help to get out is available if you need help.

Help in Houston TX

Houston Area Women Center Inc. ------------
1010Waugh Dr Houston TX 77019
 713-528-6798 Land line/ 713-528-2121 Hot line

Shelter - Aid to Victims of Domestic Abuse -------------
713-224-9911 Land line/ 713-224-9911 Hot line

Montrose Counseling Center Inc. -------------------------
401 Branard St Houston TX 77006   --------- 713-529-
0037 Land line/ (800)6990504 Hotline

Northwest Assistance Ministries --------------
15555 Kuykendahl Rd Houston TX 77090
 281-885-4555 Land line/ 281-885-4673 Hot
line

Family Affair Church Evangelical Christian
Center-- 13431 Chipman Glen Dr
Houston TX 77082
Pastor Loretta Jasper 832-845-2414

Questions you should ask before you get married

1) What should a good marriage be built on?
2) Have you been married before?
3) I need to know if your be tested for HIV?
4) I need to have a blood test?
5) I need to know if they believe in God?
6) Do you have children if so how many? Will we have children?
7) Have you been in a relationship that you were abused?
8) Did you abuse any one?
9) Do you plan to work?
10) Will you put in 100% in this marriage?
11) Where do you see your self in five years?
12) Do we eat together if so what meals?
13) Are you able to clean up with me?
14) Will we live in a house or apartment?
15) Do you have a car?
16) Why do you want to get married?
17) Do we like and respect each others friends?
18) Do we value and respect each others parents and is either of us concerned about our parent getting in our relationship?
19) Are you close to your family?

20) How much time will we spend with our families?

21) How do we settle conflicts that may come up?

22) Are you a animal lover?

23) Do you have a best friend?

24) When is your birthday?

25) Do you have any family tradition that you do around any certain holiday?

26) Do you like to travel to other cities or states?

27) How much time do you talk on the phone?

28) What do you like to do for fun?

29) How much sleep do you need every night?

30) Will we vote together?

31) Do you drink or smoke?

32) Do you like to gamble?

33) Do you know how to pray?

34) How many brothers and sisters do you have?

35) Do you love me?

36) Do you have a favorite color?

37) Do you like fishing?

38) Do I know how to shop for food?

39) What state will we live in?

We should be able to talk to about any thing when we are getting ready to be part of each others life because marriage is a big step and we must know some thing about our partner. Before, I got married I did not ask any question and that was a big mistake. I was to busy looking at his out side appearance. By looks you can be deceived looks aren't every thing. We have to look in side of our partner.

AUTHOR Loretta Jasper

The mother of three children by birth and five of her brothers children she raised as her own. I was called to preach the word of God in 2008. I never knew that God would use women as Pastors but in fact he did. I'm the Pastor of Family Affair Church Evangelical Christian Center in Houston. I am the President of Family Fight Against HIV/AIDS, Inc.-Chemical Abuse Counselor, Risk Reeducation Specialist,we provide health care education and prevention to all Ethic backgrounds in our communities. Education: Montrose Counseling Center, Red Cross (HIV Education), Health Services (DSHS) City of Houston (HIV Prevention Counseling Partner Elicitation) (PC/PE), Texas HIV Connection (WAP), Comprehensive HIV/AIDS Advocacy Training, Project Leap 2007, Health Allied LCDC. .Childcare education 30 yrs . Married now to Pastor Lee Jasper for 9 great years.

62636805R00017

Made in the USA
Columbia, SC
04 July 2019